Quin and the Jets

by Tristan Horrom
illustrated by Meryl Henderson

Decodable 12

Mc Graw Hill Education

Bothell, WA • Chicago, IL • Columbus, OH • New York, NY

MHEonline.com

Send all inquiries to:
McGraw-Hill Education
8787 Orion Place
Columbus, OH 43240

ISBN: 978-0-02-140689-0
MHID: 0-02-140689-8

Printed in the United States of America.

2 3 4 5 6 7 8 9 QLM 20 19 18 17 16 15

Quin is a Jet.

Quin is six.

Quin can run fast.

What pep!
Quin did not quit.

What a step!
Can Jan stop her?

Quin gets it in!
What a Jet!

Quin helps her Jets win!